MW01089106

Daddy Issues

Black Women Speaking Truth
& Healing Wounds

Edited By Genoa M. Barrow

**With Forewords By Ola Adams-Best, LCSW
and Flojaune G. Cofer, PhD, MPH**

Copyright © 2019 Genoa Barrow

Daddy Issues: Black Women Speaking Truth & Healing Wound

GB Unlimited Publishing

No part of this publication may be reproduced, distributed, or transmitted in any form or by any means, including photocopying, recording, or other electronic or mechanical methods, without the prior written permission of the publisher, except in the case of brief quotations embodied in critical reviews and certain other noncommercial uses permitted by copyright law. For permission requests, contact the publisher, addressed "Attention: Permissions Coordinator," at the address below.

Genoa Barrow

Daddy Issues Anthology

P.O. Box 161988

Sacramento, CA 95816

Printed in the United States of America

UNLIMITED

2019

Table Of Contents

• • • • • • • • •

Table Of Contents

• • • • • • • • • •

The Daddy Issues: Black Women Speaking

Truth & Healing Wounds anthology

is dedicated to the young lady who spoke

her own truth at South Sacramento Christian

Center and exposed the desire of her heart—

to have her father back in her life

and to have him help her

navigate her way through the pain.

Acknowledgements...

Syrai Harris (My All Day, Every Day)

She Could Be My Daughter (Dana Maeshia)

Don't Shoot Our Future Down
(Pastor Les Simmons and Berry Accius)

Eddie Robinson & The West Coast Book Team

KDEE 97.5 FM radio hosts Leon Guidry, "Smooth Jazz"
and Wanda Abney, "Full Circle"

Sheryl Lister

Eugene Redmond
(For setting the example with your Drumvoices Revue anthology.
As you always say, "Strength to Your Writing Hand!")

Contributing Writers: Kimberly Bailey, Genoa M. Barrow,
Kimberly Biggs Jordan, Bianca LaTrice Calloway,
Rev. Dr. Lillian Capehart, Sharon Chandler, Dinah Clark,
Dana Maeshia, Kathy Marshall, Naimah McDaniels,
Glynis A. Sheppard, Dorothina Shields, T.Speaks,
Denise Washington, and Angelina Woodberry.

Ola Adams-Best, LCSW

Flojaune G. Cofer, PhD, MPH

Editor's Preface

As a journalist you're taught to detach yourself from the stories you write. It's a smart lesson to learn, given the nature of some of the things we write about over the course of our careers, but it's not always possible. Sometimes the subject matter or the people involved just have a deep impact on you.

The idea for the "Daddy Issues" anthology came to me after attending an event in August 2018 titled, "Unprotected," hosted by the groups Don't Shoot Our Future Down and She Could Be My Daughter at the South Sacramento Christian Center in Sacramento, California. I was covering the event that was held in the wake of the horrific stabbing death of 18-year-old Nia Wilson at a train station in Oakland, California.

The event focused on the impact of trauma on African American women and explored how, in many ways, African American women feel unprotected in their daily lives. Motivational speaker and poet Kwabena Antoine Nixon travelled from Milwaukee, Wisconsin to Sacramento to be the guest speaker. During the "Unprotected" event, Nixon invited audience members to participate in a writing exercise where we finished the sentence, "Truth is…"

After several minutes of writing thoughts down on paper or typing them on cell phones, a few people were encouraged to share what they'd written. One woman shared how she'd done drugs and how she was ashamed to have done drugs with her children. Then, a teen girl stood and shared how she'd been sexually assaulted by a male classmate and how no one, not even her own mother, believed her, due to some past promiscuity on her part. That was rough enough for the mother in me to hear. Then she said, 'Truth is, I wish my father was still in my life.'

My heart felt for this young lady, this child who was literally crying out, trying to figure out why she'd been left to fend for herself and had so clearly been trying to create situations where she wouldn't be rejected again...looking for love, affection and attention in the wrong places and putting herself in danger in the process.

On the drive home, the young lady's emotional outburst continued to resonate with me. How many other Black girls are out there feeling alone and broken? How does a grown woman fill a void that's been a part of who she is since childhood?

It is my sincere desire to shine a light on a darkness that has long been cast on the African American community— absentee fathers and the impact it has on their daughters.

African American women were asked to share their stories, their truths, of how their father's or father figure's absenteeism or abuse (physical or emotional) played a role in how their lives have played out. Women of all walks of life responded. Their stories are different and alike at the same time...

It's not about male bashing or putting a foot in a man's back. We know that there are good fathers out there, ones who take care of their children without question and others who desire to be there and do for their children despite bad relationships/situations.

It's not about ya'll. This is about your brothers who don't get it. Those who don't see, or haven't seen until this point, the impact that their action, or lack thereof, has. It's about pulling the band-aid off the wound. It's about healing the scar and breaking the cycle. "Daddy Issues: Black Women Speaking Truth & Healing Wounds" is about moving forward, for both daughters and fathers.

Genoa Barrow
Professional Journalist & Editor

Foreword

● ●

'ACES'... The Hand That's Been Dealt

I have been known around Sacramento to give talks where I use Anakin Skywalker's progression to Darth Vader as a fictional example of childhood trauma by walking audiences through the accumulation of risk factors in his life. Notably, I start with his conception and birth. There is important context that predates his birth. By the time he's born, his father is out of the picture. The trope of the absent father has been the basis of many stories, but in the Black community it is both a dangerous and demeaning stereotype and also a reality that many children face.

There should be caution, however, in how we define absent fathers. We frequently overestimate the number of absent fathers by using marital status as a gauge of parental presence; data shows that while most Black children are born to unmarried parents, Black fathers overall are more involved in activities of daily living with their children than men of other races. And yet, the inconsistent presence or total absence of a parent does happen.

This is often accompanied by questions containing the fears and doubts of the child, namely, Why didn't he want to be in my life? Am I worthy of unconditional love?

Children rarely ask these questions directly, but they may play out in their self-esteem, behavior and relationships. The absence of a parent is part of a group of experiences in childhood known as "Adverse Childhood Experiences" or ACEs.

On October 17, 2018, Dr. Vincent Felitti, one of the original authors of the ACEs research study was honored for the 20th anniversary of the study at the biennial ACEs conference in San Francisco, California hosted by the Center for Youth Wellness. During his remarks he said, "Many of our most common and intractable public health problems are unconsciously attempted solutions to personal problems dating back to childhood, buried in time and concealed by shame, secrecy and social taboos about certain topics."

Absentee parents is often a topic that we do not treat as a trauma, nor do we openly discuss the impact it has on children. We prefer to believe "the kids are alright." And fortunately, many of them are because they have other loving adults in their life. I would be remiss if I didn't explicitly state that while the focus on absent parents is important, it is also unquestionably true that children can be successfully raised by same sex or gender non-conforming parents or extended cooperative family networks of friends and relatives. The consistent presence of loving adults of any gender who care for and protect a child is one of the most important resilience factors in a child's life.

However, for many children, the absence of a parent is experienced as a loss and accompanied by grief—except unlike other types of grief, it is unacknowledged; or if when it is acknowledged, the focus is almost exclusively on its impact on Black boys.

Taking a brief glimpse into this window of inattention and hurt was the impetus for this anthology of women's impact statements. I was on a panel at South Sacramento Christian Center in August 2018 to discuss the unprotected status of Black women in the community. During the event, attendees were asked to be honest about their intimate wishes. One young lady she wished her father was still in her life. Genoa Barrow, the creator of this anthology, was in the audience and that comment planted a seed for her to develop a collection of stories on the impact that absentee fathers have on their daughters. In the process of exploring these stories of disappointment and resilience, we will be reminded to center and prioritize the needs of Black girls.

Hopefully many of us will find solace for the girls we once were and be reassured once and for all that we are not alone, that his decision was not our fault and that we absolutely and unequivocally deserve the love we receive and so much more.

Dr. Flojaune G. Cofer
Epidemiologist

Foreword

● ●

Critical Analysis

E ver wonder why you've felt a void in your life that you just haven't been able to shake? Ever felt as if you weren't enough or not worthy of a more fulfilling intimate relationship? Have you ever felt stuck and unable to move toward your life-long goals?

This collection of stories told by African American women that have been abandoned in some way by their fathers might provide insight into your own experience. Regardless of the circumstances, the impact of being fatherless is critical as we understand the father-daughter relationship strongly influences key factors of personal development among girls and young women such as: self-esteem, confidence, interpersonal relationships, and ambition.

When I first crossed paths with Genoa Barrow, the editor and a contributor of "Daddy Issues: Black Women Speaking Truths & Healing Wounds," it was a natural synergy-- we both felt connected to one another's spirit. Bringing together a writer, advocate, community organizer and a psychotherapist demonstrated the need to share these stories. I met Genoa, who serves as the Senior Staff Writer for one of the oldest black newspapers in the country, the Sacramento Observer, after I established a Girl Scouts troop in Oak Park, an underprivileged neighborhood in Sacramento, California.

Fairly quickly in our acquaintance, I became aware of Genoa's wide range of experience having covered and written on issues relevant to the African American community for some 20 years. Yet, fueled by her passion for issues relating to women, she is committed in her future work to mentor and create opportunities for young girls to succeed. Genoa uses her work in the community as a catalyst to increase the self-esteem of young girls and to improve their chance of accomplishing life-long goals before they become subjects of her coverage.

While the research on fatherless daughters is limited in scope, Genoa's expertise, and more specifically, genuine interest and passion for issues affecting African American women and girls, has a depth that has been unmatched. In her work, Genoa is masterful at capturing the voices of the women using their words to paint the picture of their life experiences. Many of these experiences are common themes expressed antidotally by the writers with the data supporting the overarching themes on the subjects:

In 2010, approximately 75% of children within the African American community were born to unwed mothers. (Burton, 2010; Hamilton, Martin & Ventura 2010). Compare to about 24% of children for Caucasians in American (Burton, 2010)

When fathers are absent, children generally feel discarded, expelled and unlovable (Barras, 2000)

When women are unfulfilled, the family unit experiences a strain and void that can have significant ramifications for all members (Allen & Daly, 2007, Pougnet, et al 2012)

The research on this subject suggests there is overwhelming support of the notion that fathers who actively fulfill their role in the life of their child increases the likelihood for healthy, positive development and well-being (Amato &

Gilbreth, 1999; Culp, Schadle, Robinson & Culp, 2000; Harper and Fine, 2006; Williams and Radin, 1999)

As a psychotherapist, certified trauma specialist and co-principal of a private practice, I treat individuals with a full gamut of behavioral health and/or psychiatric disorders, specifically those that have experienced trauma. My work has been primarily treating women living with HIV/AIDS, substance addictions, women that have been involved in the Child Protective Services system, and women in abusive and unhealthy/unfulfilling relationships. Based on my experience and observations, a common theme among all of these women encompasses – trauma!

The authors of the stories in "Daddy Issues" are real women, like you – writing about real life experiences. Until we are able to feel free enough to discuss our life experiences, we will be held hostage to the past. Women need to know, YOU ARE NOT ALONE! The contributing writers need to know that they are not the only ones who have had the experiences that they write about in this book. The data alone support this assumption.

The stories included in this anthology are a collection of anecdotal experiences meeting clinical observations. If you've ever felt a void in your life, endured unfulfilled relationships, spent countless days and nights feeling empty, you are not alone. Working with women who have been abandoned by their fathers and seeing the magnitude of the destruction to one's self image first hand, I wonder what the outcome would be if there were supportive services earlier in childhood? What intervention would be enough to reduce the level of impairment for the client earlier in an effort to increase self-worth and self-esteem.

There are many women who have had similar experiences and it's amazing to me (yet understandable on a more rational level) that women who have been abandoned by their fathers walk through life carrying years of pain, compartmentalized to the inth degree, functioning normally from the perspective of society, working every day, taking care of their kids, and acting as a partner in intimate relationships. Yet, many yearn for the opportunity to process and make sense of the madness they feel inside.

Based on my clinical experience, there are several areas that must be addressed: first and foremost, I would encourage women to seek a culturally- competent psychotherapist. Most managed care organizations are struggling to contract with minority therapists as their clients request treatment by someone who looks like them and is knowledgeable in aspects of their culture. In most urban cities, the internet is the best resource to find a culturally competent psychotherapist. In Sacramento, the African-American Mental Health Providers (AAMHP) group offers a directory of mental/behavioral health provider listings, which includes specialty, whether providers are accepting new clients, insurance accepted and fees.

From my clinical knowledge and understanding, the key points that clients should know to overcoming the fatherless void are:

You are not the blame – Know that you are an innocent product of your parent's/parents' story. Often, you are the product of product of your parent's/parents' story. Often, you are the product of circumstance. It wasn't intentional. Many men (fatherless themselves) don't have the capacity to be an active father and that's their stuff. Refute the embarrassment. Don't claim it. Educate yourself on the facts and learn from it. We all do better when we know better.

Know the process will take time – For many women, the process of self-realization feels like a life-long journey. Often, women don't reconcile childhood trauma until well in adulthood, when they begin to notice patterns of behavior in interpersonal relationships. In order for you to be free, commit to the work that is needed, and take the time to rid yourself of your feelings of being abandoned.

Give yourself permission to feel better – You don't have to stay there, in the pain. You can accept your past for what it is and make the decision to look at your past differently. Why allow someone to impact your life and interpersonal relationships to such a significant degree when they either weren't interested enough to make a commitment to you or didn't have the ability to be there?

Define your own process – You set the rules. Don't allow others to set your course. The process of defining yourself is different for every woman. Be patient as healing takes time.

Learn to love yourself – Know that your past does not define you. You can create, or re-create, yourself and how you want the world to view you. Learn self-care methods to connect to your inner self, such as exercise, meditation and setting boundaries.

Lastly, know that I too am a fatherless daughter. I have done the work within myself and today enjoy the rewards of a loving marriage to my best friend of 42 years. I have chosen to spend my life with a man that is a full participant in our daughters' lives and feel this is the best gift that I could have ever given my daughters. Perhaps, I would not have been so focused on choosing a mate that loved children had I not been fatherless myself. I grew up with a sister from my mother and have come to know an older brother from my father and have loving relationships with both of my siblings. I am proud of who I have become despite my fatherless status.

Ola Adams-Best
Licensed Clinical Social Worker
Owner, Redefining You Therapy

WORDS OF WISDOM ·

"

*Don't forgive him.
Forgive yourself
for believing there
is something
lacking in you
because he
wasn't there.*

"

— Iyanla Vanzant

My Father's Presence

By Glynis A. Sheppard

Y ou are so much like your father!" These words, frustratingly spoken to me in my youth by my only parent, my mother, remind me of how my journey to understand "who is the other half of me" has been inspired. I needed to know what my mom meant by her statement.

My father was not in our home after I turned 2 years old. I honestly don't remember what he looked or sounded like, even though I've cried many times as I longed to know him. I didn't see photos or have conversations or visits with his family until I was an adult. I truly feel a connection, love for my father and I believe that has motivated and guided my journey in understanding myself.

As a child, I was insecure and felt unsafe many days. I saw my mother abused by men, struggle with finances and even subject us to possible abuse by others. I believe that these occurrences would have not been, had my father been there. In some ways I have been lost in my self-worth because no man ever allowed me to feel cherished and protected, as only a father can do. So, I've tried to replace him, unsuccessfully, with the wrong type of men.

I developed into an honor student, diligent white-collar worker and a determined "identity seeker." I prayed, I dreamed, I became knowledgeable of resources and of some of his family, because, I continued to ask questions. Then, answers came.

I discovered during college that because my father had been a civil service worker, I may be entitled to Social Security benefits as a student. I reached out to as many of his family members as I could, to gain required documented proof of paternity. My mother had been ill-advised to leave his name off our birth certificates. I was warmly received by my aunts and cousins. God brought miraculous connections to family who lived close by and I was able to travel to my father's hometown, meeting others who had heard of me and my only 'full" sister. I experienced a beautiful answer to my prayer to know my father when I visited my maternal grandmother.

A neighbor of hers befriended me and attempted to introduce me to a young man whose brother she was dating. As the man and I talked, I shared about my father. He said that his grandfather had visited the city where I lived and that his mother mentioned a long lost sister who was thought to live there. Well, the grandfather turned out to be my father, his mother was my sister and the man was my nephew! Thirty years later, now I know my father, through his family. He passed when I was 11 years old. And now, I know the other part of me, too. Selah!

There were many stories about my father, his other children and their mothers' and stories about his siblings. Sometimes I resented the time my step-siblings got to spend with him. I also wished I had known them, myself. It seemed that my father kept that family together as much as he could. But, his social behavior, whatever the motive, worked against his efforts. Efforts that included having a business with his brothers, caring for and supporting his sisters and being an all-around go-to patriarch.

In my acceptance/forgiveness of my fathers' absence, I've claimed some of his characteristics, both good and otherwise. I see myself as a businesswoman, with active licenses and companies. I strive to contribute to the cohesiveness of my family, by sharing my assets as well as encouraging everyone to exploit their talents. And there are many, many skills in my life experience resume, which some-

• • • • • • •

"When it comes to relationships, I'm defensive and guarded because of this missing piece. Only from books and studies do I understand that a father gives his daughter a sense of self confidence unlike anything."

times provide solutions or at least demonstrate our potential as individuals. I don't know why I have developed in this manner, but I like believing that my Speagenetic makeup has a lot to do with it. And, of course half of those genes are from my father.

Even not having known him, I love my father. That feeling allows me to love myself. And at this point in my journey, I understand better why my mother made her painfully reminiscent statement as she looked at me. I reminded her of a special person who once came into her life. I have felt frustration as she had, when a song, a phrase or a child's face reminds me of a love lost. Sometimes, it's not easy to manage such a strong feeling, especially when you are reminded by a constant presence of a person in his offspring. My talk, my walk, my thoughts, are all show my father's presence in me.

The struggle to have a good male relationship still exists for me. I still need protecting. With all my knowledge and experiences, I don't think I recognize a protector when I see one. Instead, when it comes to relationships, I'm defensive and guarded because of this missing piece. Only from books and studies do I understand that a father gives his daughter a sense of self confidence unlike anything. I've tried to fake that within myself and have fallen short every time. Men seem to know that no one is going to, or will ever, protect me. On the other hand, I'm happy to see my father in my mirror every day. I'm business savvy, because of him, a credit to my life's achievements. I'm there for every family need, as he had been for the other faction of his family. There are other great qualities in me that I deductively surmise are from him, also. I think of this "good" as a salve.

My tender place, where pains are processed into empathy for myself and others, is where I hold the emptiness of my absent father. I am grateful to God because my father's absence has allowed me to know compassion for others who may only have the opportunity to experience the presence of their father as I have mine.

Glynis A. Sheppard is 63-year-old African American woman, born in Chicago, Illinois. She earned a Bachelor of Arts degree in economics and Sociology from California State University, Dominguez Hills. She is the mother of one son and two grandsons.

Memories Of My Father

By Sharon Chandler

My only recollections of my father are of being asked to go inside and get my mother so he could beg her to stop proceedings to garnish his paycheck for back child support. I probably met him five or six times in my life, even though he only lived four miles from me my whole childhood.

Finally, when he married wife #2, did he begin regularly leaving his payment at the county courthouse. I know she had a lot to do with that. By this time I was in high school and would catch the bus every Friday after school to the courthouse to pick up my $7 check. Granted he was now making the payments regularly, but he was supposed to make a $7.50 payment. So my mother would wait a year and add up all of the 50 cents and garnish his wages again! My whole life, he never gave me anything other than those $7 checks.

I remember being in school and church programs and activities and calling to invite him to attend, but he was always too busy or made some other excuse. He wouldn't even purchase the annual Christmas cards that I sold.

My father ended up in five children-producing marriages and relationships. I am the oldest of everyone. My mother had me when she was 16 years old and he was 20. All I really know about him is from my birth certificate. As my mother's side of the story goes, when his mom found out that I was on the way, she made him enlist in the Army. My mom's mother contacted the Army and he was made to marry my mom so that he could take care of me. I guess it was a "shotgun mar-

• ⦿ • ⦿ • ⦿ ⦿ ────────────────────────

"My whole life, he never gave me anything other than those $7 checks."

riage" because they never lived together as man and wife. That lasted the stretch of his two-year enlistment.

Throughout my adult life, I would occasionally call my dad or visit him when on his side of town. We would sit on his front porch swing and he would talk about what all of his kids were doing. I introduced him to my two kids, but he could never remember their names and would refer to them as "that girl" or "that boy." I don't believe I remember him ever calling me by name either! Maybe it was just too much for him to remember, being as he had nine kids by five different women.

My whole life, I wanted to have some sort of relationship with him, but we were always uncomfortable together. I wanted to ask him why he denied my being his child when my mother got pregnant. He knew they were having sex, but I guess he knew that the age difference might have caused problems. Back in 1953, only "bad girls" got pregnant, and my mom has always referred to him as a "Momma's boy." But even so, there were plenty of years to make things right and he chose not to.

Several years before my father died of complications due to diabetes, we did have a brief discussion where he tried to explain why he failed to cultivate a relationship with me.

"Your mom and grandmother were so mean and hard on me, that I took the easy way out and just didn't want to deal with them or you," he explained. So he just took the coward's way out.

It's really funny about father-daughter relationships. They set the tone for so many relationship guidelines as we grow older. I have never fully trusted males, to be honest with me, to look out for my well being, or to take care of me. That was a great issue with my husband and our marriage. He would always remind me that I didn't have to do everything for myself anymore. I never trusted him to take care of me, even when I became gravely ill from an aneurysm. I went for a job interview only three weeks following my release from the hospital. I had to have my own money.

After having a daughter of my own, I wanted to guarantee that she would have a loving, healthy relationship with her father. Although we divorced when she was 12 years old, I never denied her talking to or visiting her father. At the age of 39, they continue to have a wonderful bond. At times, I could feel that green-eyed jealousy creeping into my eyes, as she has exactly what I never had, no matter how hard I tried. Even though we moved from the Midwest to California, my ex-husband always attended high school and college graduations, birthday and holiday celebrations, and even spent the summer as a guest at my house, while he was transitioning from jobs.

When we first separated, I could not stand to talk with him about anything. No matter how well the conversation was going, we always ended up pushing each other's buttons, ending in accusations, blame and then threats. He would always end the conversation threatening to kidnap the kids and my never seeing them again. Granted, when you are in the midst of hurt, you fail to think clearly. My mother finally pointed out to me that he was talking about kidnapping two teenagers, and what Black man is going to travel cross-country to take on the responsibility of raising two kids, he was barely taking care of in the first place? After that "get real" talk, I realized two things: from then out, I could hang up the telephone when we started arguing, and even more reasonable, I did not have to talk with him at all. The kids were old enough to make their requests for money or whatever they needed. They had a better chance of getting help from him than I. I have never figured out why men think that as soon as they are no longer sleeping with the mother of their children, the children no longer need shelter, or food or to exist.

I have a former boyfriend who swears that all of his insecurities and distrust of women and relationships stems from his mother's infidelity with his father. She cheated, divorced his father, married the man she cheated with, and then had three additional children. My advice to him: You had no control over your mother's vagina. You may have come out of it, but you certainly had no control over it.

I have learned the following lessons over my 65 years on this earth: Get over what you had no way of controlling with your dad or anyone in your life. Don't make the same mistakes your parents made with you. It's no longer about you. Our children deserve healthy, loving role models.

Sharon Chandler is the founder and executive director of Yes2Kollege Education Resources, Inc., a Sacramento non-profit dedicated to the early preparation of minority families raising college-bound students and family health and wellness. She is the mother of two college graduates, a son who is a deputy district attorney and a daughter, a human resources training professional with her master's degree in sociology. Sharon is a past executive director of community centers and affordable housing programs. She is also a former social marketing project coordinator of the CA Black Health Network's campaign against second-hand smoke, and community blogger for San Francisco Public Radio, KQED, keeping the Bay Area abreast of minority health news in South Sacramento. Sharon also has extensive experience as an advocate and writer of numerous newspaper and magazine articles on health, education, and diversity for the Sacramento Observer Newspaper/Media Group. She is the proud author of the Penguin Publishing book, "Say Yes To College: A Practical and Inspirational Guide to Raising College-Bound Kids." She is also an entrepreneur and a commissioned fine artist.

WORDS OF WISDOM

"

My father wasn't around
when I was a kid, and I used to
always say, 'Why me? Why don't
I have a father? Why isn't he around?
Why did he leave my mother?'
But, as I got older, I looked deeper
and thought, 'I don't know what my
father was going through,
but if he was around all the time,
would I be who I am today?

"

— LeBron James

If I Had A Father

By Reverend Dr. Lillian Capehart

I never knew my father. He died suddenly when I was only a year old. Both my maternal and paternal grandfathers died before I was born. I never had a stepfather, or a male sibling. A caring, committed uncle served as my surrogate father. He and his wife, my mom's sister, did not have children of their own. Everyone I knew growing up in our community had a biological father residing in their home except my sister and I. My mother and grandmother raised me.

The adage, it takes a village to raise a child is true. I was blessed to live in Oberlin Village, a community surrounded by relatives. Yet at the end of the day, there were many times when I wished my father was alive. I missed his presence at birthday parties, PTA meetings, school plays, sports, graduations, weddings and funerals. I missed my father whenever I felt afraid.

If I had a father, I would have liked to have had some serious father and daughter conversations that "kept it real," just the two of us spending both quantity and quality time in engaging interactions. My preference would have been spending quality time if only to discern if my parents were on the same page in truth and in spirit. Our dialogue would have included easy and tough questions. Would I have called him Dad or Daddy? If I had a father, I would ask him who changed my diapers and if a girl can be a lawyer and entrepreneur like he was.

I would want to know if he ever shed tears of joy or sadness. Did he ever offer a helping hand to prepare any of our southern home cooked dishes? Did he eat chitterlings? What was his favorite dessert? I would ask what his favorite book and season was and why? Did he judge others or was he treated differently for being a Black man with White skin? I would ask when was the first time he experienced discrimination as a "Negro?" Or was he racist? Did he and my mother really elope?

If I had a father I would ask him to take me camping, fishing, hiking, to any sports activity, teach me how to throw or catch a baseball and let me choose which sport I wanted to try. Would he insist I take piano lessons or buy me that accordion I really wanted? Would he rather take long ocean walks, picnic or fire up the grill? If I had a father, I'd ask what made him laugh. I'd look deep into his grey eyes and ask if he saw me in my mother's eyes, himself, or the eyes of his father? I'd search his soul and demand to know why some men cheat or abuse their wives and children?

If I had a father I would seek his advice about dating and marriage. If I had a father, perhaps I'd chatter a lot less. What would he say about when to speak up or shut up? First and foremost, I'd want to hear him tell me how much he loved me just as I am. Now if somehow he wasn't able to show and tell me this, I don't believe I would have liked him very much. Last but not least if I had a father, I would thank him for giving me life, seal it with a hug and kiss for the father I really miss. I cannot help but imagine how different my life may have been, had my father lived. Would we have remained in the South or gotten to know his relatives who traveled north and passed as White?

My mother rarely shared stories about my father who died unexpectedly. On the occasions she did, the portrait she presented seemed a bit too perfect. Unfortunately, watching the sitcom, "Father Knows Best" could only take me so far in its best attempt to navigate life as a Black female.

Truth be told my mother talked more about a "heavenly Father." Sunday morning before going to church we all gathered around the kitchen table to say several prayers. This had been a family tradition passed down by mother's own father. It always began by reciting The Lord's Prayer . . .Our father who art in heaven. . . . Mother talked openly with and to the heavenly Father. As a child, one thing was for sure, I certainly did not fully understood the meaning behind the words of this universal prayer. Whose Father was he? I did not see him as Father. Where was the Father to be found? Had my father met him? Although I could not know this heavenly Father, I grew to detect a divine presence.

As a teenager, I was chosen as one of the first three African American females to integrate Needham Broughton high school in Raleigh, North Carolina back in the day. I recall my mother's words as if spoken yesterday. "I want this decision to be yours," she said. "I'm not going to tell you that you have to do this. If something happens, I don't want you blaming me, because there is not a male living in our home."

Vivid memories of mother praying faithfully while kneeling by her bedside each day and night in silent contemplative meditation remain embedded in my head and heart. Somehow I knew a higher power led me, guided me, ordered my steps, and protected me along that painfully lonely trailblazer path. That's another story. I believed that the seed of faith was planted during this time. But I would be amiss if one was led to believe my life blossomed instantly as a bed of roses. There were indeed some serious thorns and overgrown weeds to get rid of, which is another story about forgiveness, rebirth and reconciliation. Suffice it to say that my pathway has not been an easy or predictable one.

When I reflect on my journey from the South to the North, from the East to the West, I believe that my Heavenly Father was there all along with me, even during those times when I was not following Him. Today, I am confident that my life with an omnipresent, omniscient, and omnipotent God is the best thing our Father has to offer his children. This invisible presence is within me, behind and beside me, alive and very real. I can speak to Him as friend to friend knowing unequivocally that I am loved and accepted just as I am. I know that it is really possible to talk with God and receive definite responses to prayerful questions in His perfect timing.

What matters most to me is a deep and personal relationship with God the Father as the first priority in my life, having been called to the ministry of presence and prayers. What matters even more to me is to share the good news of the gospel, and invite others to receive the blessings too of God's eternal light and love. The good news is simply that God is the Father of all people each of us, regardless of age, race, class, skin color, or income. Have we not all one father? (Malachi 2:10). The One who created me in his image and sent forth the spirit of life, his Son into my heart with a transformative compassion transcends all human understanding.

I have come too far by faith to turn back now having put the giver before the gifts. Our father who art in heaven, it is indeed a privilege to call you Father. You bridged the gaps of time and space to be present with me on earth in the absence of my human father showing me again and again, your mercy and grace in spite of my imperfections. I am confident to leave it up to you to fulfill my needs as you seem fit. I can do nothing—NOTHING— without you. I can do all things with Christ that strengthens me. What a mighty God I serve.

Wherever I am you are there with such unconditional agape love as my soul continually cries out. Abba Father you are amazing! Abba Father, all things are possible. For I am convinced that neither death, nor life, nor angels, nor rulers, nor things present nor things to come, nor powers , nor height nor depth, nor anything else in all creation, will be able to separate us from the love of God in Christ Jesus our Lord. (Romans 8:38-39) NRV

I did not know my human father, but I am glad I know who You are.

Reverend Dr. Lillian Capehart is a selfless servant of God. An elder in the AME denomination, she has served as an interfaith chaplain in hospice and hospital settings throughout the SF Bay Area. Most recently she served as solo pastor at New Vision United Methodist Church in Millbrae, California. Professional accomplishments: Educational Consultant in California Department of Education, Manager Head Start, Director of Membership for Girl Scouts. Education: BA Liberal Arts Bennett College, MA Early Childhood Ed. Wheelock College; M.Div and D.Min, San Francisco Theological Seminary.

My Truth

By Denise Washington

I missed an opportunity to have an important conversation with my estranged father. And my first question for him would have been, "Why didn't I know you?" I discovered he passed away in June of 2017, after googling his name to find him, and instead I found his obituary.

I missed him by six months and discovered I had visited near the area where he was laid to rest, during a trip to see my daughter graduate from the Air Force. I used to think that it's so important for a boy to have his father in his life, to teach him what it is to be a man and all the things I thought a mother wouldn't be able to teach him. But in our community moms have long been both parents in a child's life whether boys or girls especially in the African American household and doing a mighty fine job of it.

But what I realize is that girls might need their dads just as much, if not more than boys. I never had an opportunity to be a daddy's girl. I think I wish I had been. A dad's attention and love is what most girls base their relationships with the opposite sex on. They're kind of our blueprint for how a man should treat us, especially if you see them being kind to their daughters, wife, mother, auntie, etc. The truth is my father wasn't in my life, at least not in a way that mattered. I would see him occasionally when I would visit my grandmother during summer vacations.

I lived on the West Coast and my father lived down South. He and my mother married at an early age, they had been high school sweethearts, but were divorced only after two years into the marriage. He was quick to raise a hand to his wives and had a wandering eye. Even with that said, I still thought he was an interesting man. I didn't like his actions, but he was my father and I wanted to know him. I wish he would have taken the time to get to know me. He would have realized that I was interesting too.

He did remarry and had four children with his second wife. It was his and his wife's belief that if I wanted to know him that I should pursue him for that relationship. But as a child I could never understand why I never had him in my life. As I got older I understood the logistic part of it, but even that should not have stopped him from knowing me. And now as an adult with children of my own, I know better than to ask a child to facilitate a relationship with a parent. That should never be a child's responsibility.

I knew his name and I knew what he looked like, but I didn't know the man. If a man thinks it's OK to abandon a little girl or boy to be raised by their mother alone, they are sadly mistaken. Far too many mothers have to take on being both mom and dad. And it shouldn't be a gender thing that girls are better off in the care of their mothers; girls need their fathers too. And I'm not saying I'm bitter or that I had a bad life because he wasn't there.

I actually had a father figure in my life, I had my dad (stepdad), a man who stepped up and took on that role. He came into our lives when I was 2 years old. He married my mom when I was about four years old and I even took his name. He walked me down the aisle when I married my husband and was there for the birth of my children. That's what a dad does. It wasn't always a perfect relationship, but he was there and I appreciated that.

I do make a distinction between a father and a dad. A dad is actually around to raise you, a father is basically the one who provides the sperm. I'm in my late 50's now and I know that his absence played a role in molding me, it's affected my decision-making and how I live my life. I decided early in my life that if I had children, I wanted a two-parent household or at the very least to deal with a man who would be there for his kids. Many Black men need to step up and show integrity and character and be there for their daughters and sons, because no child should feel abandoned. There are so many ramifications of a father not being in a child's life that include emotional, physical and financial support to name a few. Black women need to be very selective about who fathers their children, because they shouldn't have to do it alone.

And for those little ones missing their fathers, it's sometimes hard, but God makes a way. I do see a change in this new generation of young Black men (Black fathers) and I'm proud of that. I'm lucky I've been married to a good man for 36 years and counting and we have four adult children. And of the four, two are men with one biological child each and taking on parenting another man's child as well. I'm blessed to say they're wonderful fathers. My daughters haven't embarked on that journey yet, but they adore their dad and he adores them, they're lucky enough to be daddy's girls.

Denise Washington was born in New Orleans, Louisiana and moved to California at an early age. She is currently a buyer for the State of California. She met and married her husband 37 years ago. They currently reside in Elk Grove, California, where they raised four children.

What I Needed Was the Freedom That Security Brings

By Dana Maeshia

I grew up around a lot of family and family friends. I was born in 1972 in San Francisco, California. My father was the son of sharecroppers and my mother was the daughter of prominent members of the church. Both of my parents migrated north to experience the warmth of another sun also known as escaping the post Jim Crow South. They had southern values and were dripping in southern hospitality. Every Sunday my childhood home was filled with folks coming to visit and break bread with my family. Our home was the center of everything, it was the place of refuge, it was the place that everyone could call home.

My dad didn't know how to read, yet he was a great provider. He honed his skills in construction and we always had a family side business. My mom, who was the nicest woman you would ever want to meet, was a nurse's assistant, a homemaker, spiritual leader, nurturer, and the matriarch of our family. My father was the figurehead with my mom creatively allowing him the leadership position. We knew, however, where the power source really resided.

I was the middle child of three girls. I had a sister 10 years older than me and one who was six years younger. I don't remember my older sister being consistently in the home and before my baby sister was born, all eyes were on me. I was the center of attention. I was adored. I was smart. I was what they called "grown," which meant I exhibited the common sense of an older person even though I was a child.

I learned early on to hide things and I remember always feeling guilty. I ingested other people's energy and as a budding empath I saw things that were not visible with 20/20 vision.

While reflecting back on all of the laughter, the sound of dominoes being slammed on my mom's dining room table, the smell of everything good cooking in the kitchen, the smiles and the numerous conversations going on at the same time, I had an awareness that everything was not OK. My parents were homeowners; in fact they owned multiple properties and often rented to other family members and close friends. Though we grew up in the hood, we went to private schools until we were bussed out.

I received a descent education up until high school. The experience of Catholic school was kind of weird because though some things sounded familiar, their way of worshiping wasn't what I was accustomed to. I was used to "weird." I was at home in that space. After private school I spent one year in the local school and that was enough to last me for a lifetime. I never had to fight so much and I was not accustomed to sitting in a class where the students were allowed to be so disruptive. When it was time to go to middle school, I was bussed out into "the Avenues," maybe an hour away from home, which was OK with me because it afforded me the opportunity to escape my reality.

By this time, crack cocaine had landed and I bore witness to it not only destroying my family structure, but whole communities. My father, and a lot of other adult males in my family, had not only tried it but allowed it to change our destiny as a family. Everything that could go wrong, did. My dad started disappearing at weird times. My mom was more tense. My dad would come home late on

• • • • • • • •

"By the time my father was allowed to come back home, I was 17 years old and had had two abortions and had a poor sense of self-worth."

payday and sometimes not at all. Everything was uncertain and somehow my environment at that time correlated with and validated what I felt on the inside all my life. Guilt, shame and humiliation. I had gotten used to the sudden changes and disappointments. Things got worse before they got better. By this time, I had learned that my big sister was not my mom's biological child. My mom was devastated when she found out that I was made aware of that fact.

I learned that my dad was less than perfect and that he was a flawed human being that had fallen victim to chemical warfare that was being waged against the Black community. During this time, my dad had extramarital affairs and my mother asked him to leave our home. Even though I was clear as to why he had to go, I secretly resented my mother for his banishment and to this day I have not totally forgiven myself.

My dad was absent for more than two years. During that time, I had started having sex with a boy from down the street who would become my husband of almost 30 years. By the time my father was allowed to come back home, I was 17 years old and had had two abortions and had a poor sense of self-worth. I was doing well in school because I had already learned what they were teaching at my high school in elementary and middle school. I was self medicating with marijuana and was lost in what I called love. The uncertainty and insecurity that had become the order of the day as a child was now pretty much sought after in my teenage and young adult life.

I was captive to my feelings and the emotions that I felt as a child. I was one with them. I wished I was able to break free of those paralyzing emotions earlier in life. Scenarios of uncertainty, however, played out over and over in my life like a broken record. Though my father is in my life now and I always believed he loved us, the three years that he was not around were pivotal. I needed him, but he was unavailable. As a result, I seem to be attracted to men who are emotionally unavailable. For this reason I have to proceed with caution and the awareness that my standards must rise to correlate with all the security and love that I was deserve. This is the backstory to my journey.

Dana Maeshia is the founder of Escape Velocity Resources Foundation, Inc. She is a mother and a community activist. A native of San Francisco, California, she has lived in Sacramento since 1994. Her favorite pastimes include business development and networking. A lover of literacy, she currently manages the Boys In The Hood Book Club, a program for young boys of color, along with Crystal Bowl Books. She also owns a few for-profit businesses and is looking forward to expansion. For more information, please contact her at (916) 710-2127 or by email at escapevelocityfoundationinc@gmail.com.

WORDS OF WISDOM ················

" Abandonment doesn't
have the sharp,
but dissipating sting
of a slap. It's like a punch
to the gut, bruising your skin
and driving the precious air
from your body.

—Tayari Jones **"**

Daddy Issues

By Dinah Clark

What does it mean to grow up without a father?

It means feeling a void, a void that only your father can heal

It means feeling like your value is conditional on how good, how liked, how well I perform, this need to be perfect for him, to prove to him that I am worthy, that I am enough

It means never quite feeling enough

It means earning two and three degrees, winning championships, titles, really succeeding in your field, yet, still feeling less than

It means comparing your life to your friend's life because she had her father, you always sort of envy her

It means attracting men who will abandon you emotionally, mentally or physically

It means not understanding men because there was no model to learn from

It means unnecessary conflicts, relationships, heartbreaks because I just didn't know what qualities to look for

It means carrying a weight around, almost like an attachment,
carrying a weight around in the form of rage…this righteous anger,
for every fiber in my being knows it is ungodly
to be abandoned, deserted

It means shoving down feelings of rejection, hurt, disgrace…
Why was I unwanted?

It means being a grown ass woman, yet in small, interstitial spaces deep
within the soul, there resides a little traumatized girl

It means building up a wall to protect yourself from
potential men and women
who may abandon you, only to realize you have become a prisoner
inside of these walls of "protection"

It means having a soul wound

It means loving a man, yet being terrified that he will leave,
just like your father

It means praying, hoping, raising your son to be different
from your own father

It means turning into a little girl every time you hear from him,
even if you're 33

It means writing a poem titled, "Black Man I Noticed" and reciting it on
Facebook, and having your dad call you apologetically, he still has regret

It means being robbed of your first superhero

It means dating a man who is a wonderful father
and being slightly jealous of his kids…

Damn, I wish I had a father like you

It means being in pain

It means having to be strong, only to realize that I am weak

It means you're about to cry while writing or reading this poem

It means healing, and moving through worlds of hurt,
forgiving and forgetting

It means unlearning and unpacking your shit

It means being determined to be free of your

Daddy.
Issues.

Dinah "Miss Deliverance" Clark is one of five children, born in Dallas, Texas. At the age of two, her parents divorced. She attended middle and high school in Stockton, California, where she currently resides. Dinah is an active poet, teacher and writer. In May 2018 she authored her first book titled, "Words Are Real: An Interactive Book of Poetry." Dinah has master's degrees in both ethnic studies and education and teaches high school English. She has a 4-year-old son named Alexander. Dinah performs in open mics and poetry showcases and she loves sharing her words with her students and her community.

Locked Up Love

By Naimah McDaniels

I'm trying to write my thoughts down but these tears keep dropping from my face onto the paper, causing me to pause and gather myself together so that I could continue. It's an all too familiar feeling, as I am often trying to gather myself together so that I can continue to face the world on a daily basis.

Sometimes I feel so empty and helpless searching for something I never had, which was love from a healthy, loving father in my home. My situation was completely different from most. I was conceived during a conjugal visit and I grew up visiting my father in prison. So yes, my situation was completely different from others, at least that's how I felt growing up.

No one in my circle had a father who was incarcerated and it wasn't to be discussed. My mother told us it wasn't to be discussed, so I kept it to myself. The hard part about having a father who was incarcerated wasn't just throwing kissing through a glass window or not being able to hug him at times, it was visiting him and having to leave. I remember driving away from the prison and being in the backseat of the car staring out the back window crying in silence, wishing he could home with us and not fully understanding why.

Damn it, here come the tears again.

It was like I had a father but I didn't. I missed that presence of a man. That's not to downplay my mother, because she did what she could, but she wasn't a man nor was she my father.

I truly feel like I'm affected 'til this day from his absence. My mind knows what

I want in a man, or what I should have, but my heart is fucked up. It seems like the older I get, the worse it is. I never had an example of a relationship in the home. I have had men that were amazing, but I didn't realize that. I thought they were "too nice" or "too corny" or that I wasn't "good enough" for them because they didn't have the same similar upbringing as me. My heart was so fucked up. It's like asking an adult to read a book and they never learned how to read. How am I supposed to know what type of man to choose? My choices in men were the ones that came from single family homes as well, or controlling men, insecure men, unstable men. Players and momma's boys.

"My mind knows what I want in a man, or what I should have, but my heart is fucked up."

My heart has been broken a million times and scattered like a puzzle. I truly believe that it's due to the absence of a loving father that I attract those individuals. I was looking for something, or someone, to put the pieces together. I can't change my past, but what I have learned, which is extremely hard to do, is Love Thy Self--to get the key to unlock and release all that holds me back, gathering my own pieces and teaching myself what love is. I know that I deserve a loving healthy relationship that's free, unlocked and healthy. Who doesn't?

It is time for me to speak up and speak out about this. As Dr. Maya Angelou once said, "There is no greater agony than bearing an untold story inside you."

Naimah McDaniels, aka Ms. Moon, is a 40-year-old African American woman and mother of two beautiful children. Born in Sacramento, California, Naimah graduated from Valley High School in the Class of 1995 and then continued her educational path at Grambling State University where she received her bachelor's of science degree in the field of recreation therapy. She is currently a recreational therapist with the California Department of Corrections.

The Fatherless Daughter

Traits Inherited From An Absent Father That Helped Me Heal From The Past

By T.Speaks

I didn't have a father growing up. I didn't have a picture of him, never received a phone call from him, a letter, a family of origin, a keepsake, nothing. I don't have his date of birth, his mother or father's name, the names of his siblings or that of any other children he might have. I have nothing from him, but his name. I have his name that is on my birth certificate and I am not even sure is the right one.

I tried locating him several times throughout my young adult life. I was even called in by the County to take a DNA test for someone whom they thought might have been my father. But like Maury would say to this man and myself in the results letter mailed to us weeks later, "You are NOT the father!" Imagine how devastated I must have been, thinking that after all of these years of not knowing, that I had come this close to meeting my biological father and it turns out, he's not the one. So the person named on my birth certificate as my father had no true value to me, it was just a name.

Which is why I was so eager to change my maiden name at the ripe young age of 21, by marrying a man 19 years my senior. I wanted a man to love me so much that I was willing to settle for the first man to tell me he loved me and had the financial means to court me. We married, had our daughter and were divorced all within the same year. I could not ignore the physical and psychological abuse that layered our short-lived union and so I was broke, broken hearted and a single mother by the age of 22. The unfortunate part of life is that women really do marry their fathers. Since my father was absent all of my life, I married someone who was emotionally and physically absent. I married a con artist who was a wolf in sheep's clothing. I was his prey. A poor little Black girl with daddy issues and no real family to protect her from the snares of real life. My ex-husband took advantage of me and I almost lost my soul staying in an abusive, toxic marriage that only added to the pain and betrayal I felt from not having a father there to warn me against guys like that. I seethed with anger and bitterness as I went through the divorce process and transitioned into a full-time, working, single mom.

My story is not uncommon and that is the most unfortunate part of this. I often wonder how we have so many Black men walking around and some of them do not even have a relationship with the children they brought into this world. For whatever reasons they have, whether it be the relationship with the child's mother is strained, they have mental health or addiction issues, they just do not want to be engaged in their children's lives, etc. etc. There's no remedy for the lifetime of pain that is bestowed upon the fatherless child, especially the fatherless daughter.

It is not my intent to bash the Black man, shame them for their faults or ridicule them for making excuses for not being present in the lives of their offspring. I'm shining a light on my story, which others may relate to, to offer hope to any fatherless daughters who suffer in silence year after year from not knowing who their father is or not having a healthy relationship with him. I want these fatherless daughters to see my story, and that of others, as an invitation for them to explore their own truth and accept healing from their authentic self so that they may go out and spread that healing for others to receive as well. That is the only reason I am sharing my story, to spread healing to others who are just like me.

I struggled with wanting to regurgitate the emotions and feelings of still not having a father or not even knowing who the hell he is in my 33rd year of life.

Sometimes I look at myself in the mirror and become ashamed of who I am. I see a beautiful, vibrant young Black queen, but feel the emptiness of a little girl who is looking outside her window waiting for her father to show up and he never comes. He just never, ever comes.

The little girl grows up thinking to herself, "Well, I will just be perfect at everything and maybe if I'm a good person and do everything right, my dad will notice and come home." The little girl in me tries really hard to people please and overcompensate in life and try to be perfect at everything, in hopes that my father will suddenly knock on the door and say, "You did it Princess! You're perfect enough so now I can come home! Now I can reveal myself to you and we can be a happy family. I will tell you why I was gone for so long. I'll wipe your tears away and take you out for ice cream. I'll buy you a purse, help you choose your husband and be there to protect you always and forever. I will never, ever leave you again!" I know, I know… magical thinking right?

Let me tell you what traits I've inherited by having an absent father and how I've learned to heal myself, and continue to heal daily. *1.* Love yourself first and always be selfish. Yes, my father taught me that he loved himself first and was selfish enough to walk away from this precious baby unicorn (Me! And to the women reading this, you are the precious unicorn, too!). My father was not good enough to raise me and so he did me a favor by walking away from me as soon as I was born. He taught me that I have to take care of myself and put my needs first above all others or I will always get the short end of the stick. As the old saying goes, no one can love you better than you. *2.* Actions and consistency over a long period of time will determine a person's character. I had no idea what to look for in a potential spouse because I did not have a father growing up to show me consistency, actions, character traits, etc. etc., and so I did not have a blueprint for what a "man" looks like. This is even assuming that if I had a father around, he would be a good one, right? I swear, it's like rolling the dice with some of these men sometimes! You never know what you are going to get.

I say all of this to say, in my dealings with men, and people in general, you have to see them over a long period of time and base their actions and consistency on whether or not they are a true match for you. Not growing up with a father has taught me to stay neutral and detached from the process of getting to know people. People have their ups and downs and are entitled to bad days but it is the consistency over time that allows me to make a conscious decision as to whether or not I'm going to "mess with them the long way" so to speak.

Thanks Dad, for teaching me to keep my cool and give people time to show their true intentions and character before I fall head over heels for them and make them an honorary family member! 3. Build confidence by getting in physical shape, paying off debt, and saying "no" to things that no longer serve you. How productive could I be in my own personal journey if I always reminded myself I did not grow up with a father nor do I even have a point of reference of who he is? What good am I doing by replaying the vision of the heart break with violin music of the little girl sitting in the window waiting for her father to show up but he never does? How does sitting in sadness and pain serve me over the long haul? I think you know where I am going with this one. It does not! It simply does not serve me at all.

My father taught me that I really do have to brush the dirt off my knees, along with the sting of his rejection, and keep it moving, baby. He was not worried about my little girl feelings or the impact of not having him in my adult life now, so why should I live in the past and give someone my energy who was not even around to help foster and develop it? I know what you are thinking, "It is easier said than done," and you are absolutely right. But, once you are done stewing for five min-

• • • • • • • •

"My father taught me that I really do have to brush the dirt off my knees, along with the sting of his rejection, and keep it moving, baby."

utes in the corner over not having a healthy father figure around to help you navigate this toxic world and all of the patriarchal double standards us women go through, dry your eyes, go to the gym, sweat it out, pay off some bills and keep going!

Not having a father has its perks. It allows me to be brutally honest and matter of fact about my situation which means I get to own the outcome and not give him or anyone else credit, or blame, for the decisions I make. 4. Surround yourself with winners and not losers. This one is simple. My father was a loser and that is why he left. I'm not mad that he is a loser. I am mad that it took me 33 years to realize he is a loser. So I can decide to stew on not having a loser in my life or I can make amends and get around some winners and start winning at life! Get around some winners and they will make you forget you ever had a loser in your life because they will be so busy helping you win, there will be no time in the day to discuss loser shenanigans. 5. Always remember that if you make it to adulthood, you have already won. 6. Your future self depends on you. In moments of doubt, ask yourself, "What would my future self want me to do?" I think about what my 43-year-old self would tell my 33-year-old self. She would say, "Get your life and don't stew over that loser father!" 7. Have fun. Life is so brutal and mundane. I think we can get caught up in the past and what we did not have growing up, how we wish things were different, etc. etc. We need to have fun and break up the routine. My father taught me to have fun. Obviously he had (a lot) of fun with my mother and left her with the hard part of raising me. I laugh because I know my mother would have still let my father slide through even if she had known he would leave. She was just that type.

I may have started off rainy and cloudy but I hope I painted a clear picture that growing up without a father is indeed, tremendously emotional. The gaping hole in my heart will probably never be filled, but the holes in my game, when it comes to my approach to life, can be filled with fun, reflection and taking ownership over me. I'm always encouraged when I do the personal development work that is needed because it offers healing. But more importantly, not having a father no longer owns me, I do.

T.Speaks, aka Toni Lockett, is an author, fitness model, public speaker, mother, and founder of "Understanding The Black Man." Her hobbies include amateur boxing, hosting speaker panel events, and writing short stories. Her mission is to help heal the Black community and create thriving Black businesses that will benefit future generations. T.Speaks is the author of "Someone Lied To Me! How Come No One Told Me The Truth About Life?" She can be reached at UTBM.2018@gmail.com

WORDS OF WISDOM ················

"
Fathers,
if your presence
makes a difference,
trust me, your absence
makes a difference.

—Reverend Dr. Rich Schuhmeier

"

Pieces Of Me

By Angelina (A-Jae) Woodberry

Memories of my life before 1981 are scattered like a 100-piece puzzle on a table that doesn't have a picture of what it should look like on the box. That December, shortly before Christmas and after the second grade had ended for winter break, my grandmother moved us from the foggy cliffs of Daly City, California to the foggy valleys of Sacramento, California's capital city. Our new home sat on the edge of a cul-de-sac in a small, newly built section of tract homes that butted up against a bright red, steel railroad fence. I quickly became friends with the only two other children living there. They both lived with their mothers and fathers.

Mothers, I knew about and even had a few in my life. My biological mother, who spent most of her educational career in a small Catholic school, had won the argument with her adoptive mother and father to attend public high school. There, as a freshman, she met a senior who preyed on her innocence and soon became pregnant. More concerned about the way an unwed teenage mother would affect her social status, my grandmother quickly convinced my mother and the father to get married and raise me. Within the first three years of my life, I had gone back and forth between my grandmother's Daly City home and the San Francisco projects. Courtesy of undiagnosed mental illness, cultural differences, substance abuse, and being too young to be married with a child, that marriage didn't last long.

A court battle ensued and after several people in suits, judges in robes, and tears on all sides, custody of my four-year-old self was given to my mother's parents.

One of the only stipulations, I would come to learn about 10 years later, was that the father and his family was to have no contact with me. None. No cards, calls, or even smoke signals. None. Fearing repercussions from the court or my grandfather's .410, the father obeyed the order. By the time I was five, cancer had eaten up my grandfather's liver. Diagnosis, hospital and funeral; all in what seemed like a matter of months. Another father figure gone.

Growing up, the puzzle pieces continued to selectively fit into place. As years passed, my memories of the father faded like cool mist in the warming sun. Watching other fathers with their daughters, I felt hollow inside. Something was missing. I would see other families together and long to have one like theirs. A mother who went to work and a father who did the same. A father who would spend time with his children and participate in their lives. Girls look to their fathers to learn how men should treat them in the world. It's a vital part of the growing up process. I learned that growing up without half of yourself was difficult.

Without access to the biological father, I attached to other fatherly figures in my life. When I was around seven, my mother began dating a man she had met in Catholic middle school. I would often go to the park and the zoo with them. He was an important part of my life for several years. That all changed when my mother and her boyfriend had my brother. Sadly, my relationship with my brother's father also changed. Some men treat their biological children different than their stepchildren. Even if it wasn't readily obvious to everyone else, I felt it and the hollow deepened. Throughout my teen years, various male role models tried to fit in that space. Some came close, but none quite fit perfectly.

Dating in high school was challenging. Looking back now, at the string of older guys I went out with, I can see how I tried to find that missing piece. Those relationships were Flint water toxic. During this time, my mom had left my stepdad, he had remarried and had his own daughter. We grew further apart. That was just as much about my jealousy as it was him not knowing how to reach me. I was an adult with children of my own before my stepdad and I ever began to form some sort of connection. It was his wife who helped cultivate that. Despite knowing him the majority of my life, it was still awkward. This man that had no biological imperative to care about me—yet he did— and was there when I needed him. Over the years we have developed a bond that is truly unique. I am grateful that he is in my life. But still, the puzzle had a missing piece.

After a string of failed romances, I met the man would eventually become my husband. Throughout our entire courtship, he was curious about the father and that part of my family. He was the only one. My bitterness would not allow me to even entertain the idea of him. My husband was certain that there was more to the story. After some effort he left a slip of paper on my nightstand one morning before he left for work. It had the father's name on it and the location of where he was. I threw it away. If he didn't want me, then I didn't want him.

The first time I saw my husband holding our baby girl, the familiar pangs of jealousy hit me suddenly and pierced my sides like Roman soldiers to a dying Jesus. She would have what I never did. She would have a Rock Her To Sleep, Comfort Her When She Is Scared, Teach Her How To Ride A Bike, Take Her To The Zoo And Father Daughter Dances daddy. I chose my spouse partially based on how he was with his various nieces and nephews. I knew that he would be a great father, and he has been to our daughter, son and me. Through his example of unconditional love and unwavering support, I learned how to trust and be comfortable with expressing the real me without fear of rejection.

A few years ago, my husband came barreling into the bedroom to interrupt my intense "Game of Thrones" marathon watching by grabbing the remote and pausing it. Looking at him like he had lost his mind, I started to ask him what he was doing, when he showed me his phone. There, on the unnecessarily large screen, was a message from a woman claiming to be an auntie. Still not interested, I looked at him, grabbed the remote and went back to Westeros. Knowing how stubborn his wife was, he left the room in quiet defeat. Weeks later, he and our daughter attended a father-daughter dance at her school. When they returned, I saw the video of how they had won a quiz show-style game of Who Knows Their Daughter Best. He got every one of the 10 questions correct. He knew her favorite color, song, artist, sport, TV show, movie, food, drink, etc. He knew everything about his little girl. The ugly green-eyed monster stormed into my feelings. I wanted to be someone's little girl. I wanted someone to know everything about me.

It was time to follow up on this auntie and my husband agreed. I spoke with my stepdad, who I had remained somewhat in touch with through the years. I also spoke with my spiritual father, our pastor, to seek advice on how to proceed. They were both very reassuring and supportive. Having had challenges in the past with their own fathers, they understood my hesitation. It still took me several months after that to gather enough courage to contact the auntie. With some fear and trepidation, I messaged her on Facebook. We had a few really nice exchanges. I learned about her and her son. I was told that I have two sisters, both younger than me, and three brothers, one older and two younger. She didn't say, and I didn't ask, but I wondered what type of father he was to those children. Why did he want them and not me? I think it would have broken every piece of me to find out that he wanted them and not me. I never shared these fears with her, but she seemed to sense them. She told me how the family had always remembered me. All my siblings and cousins knew about me. My birthday was even celebrated every year. Then she sent me a picture of the father. As I stared for what seemed like hours at this stranger, I could see parts of my daughter's smile in his face. I could see his eyes on my son. What I couldn't, wouldn't, or didn't want to see was any part of me in him.

As far as I was concerned, we were nothing alike. I would never leave my children. I'd fight a whole naval fleet to stay with them. How could he not feel the same way about me? How dare he not fight for me, I thought. Despite my animosity, I agreed to come to Thanksgiving dinner in a few weeks with the family. As the time drew nearer, I wished my mother were alive to join me. It would have been nice to have her as a buffer to build whatever was going to be cobbled together. The time came, the long drive to the Bay Area was at an end. My husband texted the auntie to let her know we were there. She came out of the house with her sister and a cousin. They cried and hugged me and told me how long they had been looking for me.

I was numb. Looking for me? I was the easiest person on the planet to find. I had googled me several times and always found me. They couldn't have looked too hard, I surmised. Then they led me to the kitchen of the house on the lip of the cul de sac. The room was full of brown faces, some young, some old, some neither. The stunned silence was deafening and no one said a word. I'm not sure if it was because they were unable to or didn't have the words to say anything. The older auntie called her brother's name. He turned around and the color of this cocoa complexion quickly faded. My husband later described it as if he'd seen a ghost. He came forward with tears streaming and embraced me saying "oh my baby girl." And in that instant, every fear, every shred of anger and nervousness quickly fled my body like roaches scattering when the lights come on. In my daddy's arms I felt love, warmth and acceptance. I felt the edges of the puzzle piece snap into place and complete the picture.

When a person grows up with a father, the relationship develops and matures organically. When a father is thrust into your life as a 38-year old grown, married woman with two children, the relationship isn't as natural. I have struggled over the past four years with how to build that relationship. I use the excuse of having a busy life to justify why I don't reach out more. Understanding how difficult this is for me, my dad has never pushed or been upset with me about it. I honestly don't have any anger toward him. He answered all my questions about why he left and never tried to find me. He figured that my grandparents, being rather well off, would do a better job taking care of me than a 21-year-old kid from the projects. He too was afraid of being rejected.

Looking back on it a few years later, I like the picture. I still haven't figured out how to frame it or where to hang it in my life, but I like it.

Angelina (A-Jae) Woodberry is a Bay Area-born storyteller that draws upon the experience of life to colour her fiction. The award-winning author has published short stories, poems, and academic and personal reflective essays in several literary journals over the past two decades. A children's play she wrote was performed by a local theater company. She has also served as editor on various educational texts. A-Jae lives in Sacramento with her husband and two teenage children.

His Loss...

By Genoa M. Barrow

"Don't ever contact me again." It's not exactly what a woman wants to hear from a man right after she's given birth to his child, but that's exactly what I got.

A dial tone echoed in my ear, sounding as cruel as the words themselves. As I lay there in the hospital bed, the phone turned cold in my hand and I felt chilled to the very core of my soul.

How on earth had I gotten here? He'd promised that he would be there, that history would not repeat itself, that he wouldn't "leave me out there like that." But there I was, very much alone with a newborn baby. The man that I'd trusted far more intimately than any other was now telling me that he didn't want to be bothered, that he wouldn't be bothered.

A haunting sense of deja vu came over me. Was this how my mother felt almost 30 years before, when my own father walked out on her upon learning that she was pregnant with me?

It's the ultimate rejection to have the person who is half responsible for your very existence turn their back on you, to walk away before even meeting you. That action, that choice on my father's part, said that I wasn't worth it; that he didn't want to be there when I was born, that he didn't want to cut the umbilical cord while cooing at me in a silly voice and promising to be the best daddy ever, my protector. It said that he didn't want to cradle me in his arms and promise to give me the world or die trying; that he didn't want to show me off to his relatives, about how cute I was or how smart I was.

His absence spoke volumes, yet we suffered in silence. It was something that we never, ever spoke about. There had to be pain there, though. My mother has only ever mentioned my father vaguely, as part of some snippet about her younger days, but no real, tangible information. I first saw his name on some legal papers she'd filled out, and even that was suspect, as she hinted to later finding out about some subterfuge on his part while they dated. She also never spoke ill of him or maligned him for leaving her to raise his child on her own-- not once. I would have thought she would have at least once or twice since I've been alive, but when I say never, I mean never.

Growing up, not having a father was "normal." I was raised in a neighborhood where it was "normal" to see Black and brown mothers raising their children solo. They swallowed their pride, and pain, and did what they had to do in order to make up for the fact that there was no father in the household. They struggled. They had other relationships and may have even married someone else, but those men often treated the women's offspring differently because they were indeed, "some other man's child."

I think it was normal for me to, as a young girl, wonder from time to time if my father ever thought about me. It's like that Brian McKnight song, where he asks 'Do I ever cross your mind? Any time?" Did my father count me when people asked him how many kids he had? Did he secretly watch me from the edges of my neighborhood as I played in the park or the jungle gym at school? Did he wonder what I looked like, if I had his eyes, his nose? People often say I look like my mother, but what parts did I get from him? I knew he never sent any money, because we were super poor, living in the projects and some support from him would have clearly made a difference. I didn't dream of Barbie dolls and frilly-dresses. I yearned for food that you didn't buy with color-coded "stamps" and clothing that didn't come from a thrift store or the clearance pages of the Sears catalogue. Often fathers who don't take care of their children argue that they're only seen as a payday or paycheck by the mothers of their children, or their children. I believe that it's the responsibility of both parents to make sure a child has what he or she needs. You eat every day and wear clothes every day. You find money for those things. To leave a child of your own creation without is unexcusable to me. The number of men nowadays trying to threaten or sweet talk women into taking them off of child support sickens me.

I hear it from women I know personally and on a television show that I'm currently obsessed with, "Paternity Court." Mothers come to prove that men are the fathers of their babies. Men come on to prove they aren't. Adults also come to settle decades-old paternity mysteries. I'm not one typically to air out my business for the whole world to see and I can't stand the way many men dog the women they've had relationships/relations with, but I can't stop watching. Maybe it's because somewhere deep down inside, I dream of my dad being one of those older gentlemen who come back into the picture years after the fact, genuinely wanting to apologize for not being there and wanting to make up for lost time.

Off the top though, I'd never, ever allow him to cast aspersions on my mother's character the way some of the men who come on the show do before it's determined by DNA Diagnostics that they are indeed the father. Maybe I just watch "Paternity Court" for the same reason most folks watch "reality TV"— to reassure myself that there are people out there who are more messed up than me.

There were a few times in my early years when I wondered if my father ever called my mom and asked to see me or for her to send him pictures, or was he that cruel, that unfeeling, to just not give a damn, to never give me another thought? I quickly decided on the latter and convinced myself that I didn't care. He became a non-factor in my life, just as I was in his. If he didn't care, I didn't either. I created an aura where nothing phased me and my whole demeanor screamed, "You ain't got to like me." It's armor that I still protect myself with today.

That first rejection followed me throughout my life. As a child, I looked at men that came into my mother's life with a side-eye. What do you want and how long are you going to stay after you get it or don't get it? As an adult, I overlooked BS in relationships, not wanting to say anything that would make a man leave, when I should have spoken up about the BS, so he would leave. Whenever faced with rejection, either personally and professionally, I revert back to that little girl me who was left to wonder if she'd ever be good enough. You can tell yourself that hey, that opportunity wasn't meant for you, that a particular relationship wasn't what you needed, that it wouldn't have worked out in the long run anyway, but there's always that tiny feeling inside that it was you, not them.

Some have suggested writing my feelings out in a journal and then burning it, as a way to bring about closure. At this point in my life, I don't think it, or he, is worth the effort, if I'm really being honest.

I have a good friend who wrote her father a long letter once, outlining how their relationship had been, what it had dwindled down to and how she wanted and needed to rekindle their former closeness. It was a genuine, heartfelt outpouring of love and raw emotion from an adult daughter to her beloved daddy. I remember her reading it to me over the phone and crying inside for her and wanting the letter to touch her father as she intended it to, as she needed it to. I also cried a bit for myself, because there will never be a letter that I can send, in hopes of my words and feelings taking hold in my father's heart and getting him to see what impact he had on my life, to see what he was missing by not being there.

A few years later, I thought of that letter as my friend's father walked her down the aisle at her wedding. She'd gotten her daddy back and it was, and is, a beautiful thing.

"There will never be a letter that I can send, in hopes of my words and feelings taking hold in my father's heart."

A daughter shouldn't have to beg her father to be a part of her life. A woman shouldn't have to beg a man to be in his child's life.

This became crystal clear to me around the time my daughter was about two years old. I was being honored for my contributions to the field of journalism and my daughter's father showed up to the event. I hadn't seen him since before I'd given birth. He showed up and so did what I refer to as my "Black girl." She's not the calm, cool, good-natured woman I display to the world on most days, but the chick that was born and raised in West Oakland and Richmond and dares you to test her patience.

How dare he show up to "my event" and not even acknowledge our child, who had been sitting on my lap, as cute as she could be, wearing a pretty little purple dress my mother had bought for her. So I was going to make him say something. I took her little hand and headed straight for him. He bolted. She thought it was a game.

"The man is running," she said, laughing. "We chase him."

That stopped me dead in my tracks. I asked myself, "Why am I chasing his

Black ass?" I decided right then and there that I shouldn't have to, that she shouldn't have to. And I could have stayed in that maligned space, where once again I felt rejected, but ultimately it wasn't about me, it was about my child, and giving her what I never had, a father who was present and active in her life.

Like my mother, I never said negative things about my child's father in her presence. When she was small and other people spoke ill of her father in front of her, I'd walk away so that she didn't have to hear it and be negatively influenced by anything other than his own actions. Over time, I began to foster a relationship between them. She knows who he is and who her people are. It's important for a young person to have a knowledge of self, a sense of family, of connectedness. A lot has gone down since those early years and their relationship is still fractured. But at least the opportunity to build and grow is still there. That's something I never had. I recently got an apology from my child's father for some things that were said and done in the past and I accepted that in the spirit in which it was given. I likely won't ever get that from my own father and I've accepted that . Father-daughter relationships can't be forced. Being there goes a long way. All I know of my father is that he walked away and didn't look back. I don't know any different because he has never been around to tell me any different. His choice, not mine. *His loss, not mine.*

"Daddy Issues" publisher Genoa M. Barrow is a mom first and foremost. She writes for the Sacramento Observer newspaper and her byline has appeared in publications across the country. Genoa is a founding member of the West Coast Book Team, an online support site for authors and publishers. She also raises money annually for breast cancer survivors. In her "spare" time, she's an avid reader and loves watching movies and television shows that are adapted from books. "Lord of the Rings" "Game Of Thrones" and "Queen Sugar" are among her favorites.

Daddy Hunger

By Dorothina Shields

"Who's your daddy?"

you whisper in my ear,

I don't know,

I am starving,

I swallow the thought.

"You are!"

I scream,

Burrowing my face into your chest,

Gripping your arms tightly,

I want you to stay with me here,

Where nothing else matters, but you and I

Together, like this

Your body, covering my body,

We are soft, warm, light

You lift me up,

I wrap my legs around

You and I

Look into your eyes,

You kiss me on my forehead,

Then on my lips. I feel full.

You whisper, "Baby I've got to go." Again,

I feel empty.

I don't want you to leave

tears fill my eyes,

Silence lays me down.

I reach for your hand-- loving, willing,

You hold me for a little while,

Then you leave. You always leave

Me, hungry. Waiting, wanting.

Dorothina Shields is an elementary school teacher working at a public charter school in Sacramento, California. She has been writing poems, short stories and screenplays since she was eight years old.

WORDS OF WISDOM

" Moms and dads don't last forever.
If you've got unfinished business,
we need to face that,
and that's not easy.
Every child wants to love
their mother and father.
Love is the most important thing,
and when they feel rejected
and unloved,
that hole can never be filled
by anyone else.

— Goldie Hawn

"

Acceptance of Five Words

A Fatherless Daughter

By Bianca LaTrice Calloway

Realization. *I am a fatherless daughter.* It has taken me 42 years to finally acknowledge and accept those five words. What took so long for me to say five words that would have such tremendous influence on my life and related choices?

Acceptance. As a teenager, I recall watching the "Dr. Phil" show when he would tell guests that, "You cannot change what you don't acknowledge." I did not fully understand that statement until later in my adult life after heartbreak, domestic abuse, rejection, and trust issues. I found myself wondering why I needed to acknowledge something I did not ask to have. I did not create this notion of fatherlessness that would eventually cause me to unconsciously seek acceptance and validation from others.

Defense mechanism. In retrospect, when the subject of fatherlessness would come up in conversations, I did not feel that it related to me in any way. Maybe I made myself believe that having maternal grandparents, GiGi and Papa, actively in my life somehow filled the void of being fatherless. After all, what did my life really look like as a daughter without a father? Through the lens of a 7-year-old girl, I did not feel the effects of his absence. My mom always shared stories and pictures of when he lived in our household, until when I was a toddler, he and mom divorced. I did not feel fatherless because I knew who he was, his birthdate, the names of his other estranged children and, on occasion, maybe once or twice every other year, he would pop up at our house unannounced. I did not understand the impact it had on me with him being occasionally present, yet always emotionally absent. The only family picture I knew of was my mother, my maternal grandparents and my two older sisters; they had a different dad.

Reflection. If I had to recall my best memories of my dad, it would be the few times he did come to our home. I remember one particular time like it was yesterday. He was sitting in our kitchen while my mom's friend applied a Jheri Curl to his hair. There were also the times he would have my sisters and I sit at the kitchen table while he taught us how to play the game of backgammon. Let me not forget the time he popped up early one morning to take me with him to sell his homemade fragrance oils and incense sticks at Denio's flea market. I was so mad that he showed up, let alone on a day there was no school and I could sleep in. I guess he wanted to teach me the principles of being an entrepreneur. Needless to say, I was not feeling like an entrepreneur. I felt more like an agitated teenager who had to get up way too early on my Saturday.

I learned to accept his occasional good deeds, so it is of no surprise that this acceptance influenced my relationship decisions. At an early age, I did not realize I was being raised by what society referred to as a single mother. I just knew I had all the love and material things that most children desired. Mom, GiGi and Papa were actively involved at my school and recreational activities. Again, I did not realize my father's presence, or lack thereof, was an issue in my life until I was a college freshman.

Courage. During summer break in 1995, I mailed a handwritten letter to let my father know that I believed I was feeling the impact of his absence. I wanted him to know that although I did not understand his reasons for being inactive, I forgave him and wanted to build a healthy father-daughter relationship. Two weeks later he called me to chat about my letter. To my surprise and disappointment, without going into specifics, that phone call concluded with my dad (who is African American) saying he was not sure what I wanted from him because he believed in the "American philosophy of fatherhood." Huh? Ouch and wow! I didn't know then and still have no idea what that means or if such a thing exists.

Rejection. It took me several days to muster up the courage to write such an emotional letter in that moment of vulnerability. I hadn't expected that I would end up feeling totally crushed by his response. From that moment forward, I knew I wanted a relationship with a man who was the total opposite of my father. I knew I desired to one day marry a man who was nothing like him. I prayed for a man who would love me unconditionally, would be physically and emotionally present and who would have a strong, loving presence in our household once we started our own family.

Pressure. Did my broken relationship with my dad impact my relationship decisions? Absolutely yes, without a doubt. There were red flags I ignored and behaviors I accepted in my marriage that clearly stemmed from not wanting to "lose" another man in my life. Afterall, I had placed the pressure on myself to break the cycle of divorce and raising children in a single-parent household. So, when those red flags appeared in my relationships and marriage, I thought I could pray them away.

Emotional dishonesty. The notion of emotional dishonesty is a term I heard Iyanla Vanzant use when she appeared on "The Oprah Winfrey Show" many years ago. Not being honest with the pains of the past stemmed from being a fatherless daughter. I ask myself, how would I know to accept something I had never really faced?

Victimization. I did not want to use being fatherless as a crutch and an excuse that would block me from being a hopeless romantic. It literally frustrates me to see people use the lack of a parent as their reasoning for not succeeding in life. So, I guess I feared that acknowledging the pain of being without a father would automatically thrust me into the victim category.

Influence. I am a fatherless daughter. Those five words are part of my life's journey. I refuse, however, to let being fatherless create the blueprint for my life and my related choices. Does being fatherless explain some decisions I have made and behaviors I accepted from men? Yes, they do, however, thanks to having a strong, independent mother and a relationship with my heavenly Father, I acknowledge and now accept the absence of my father in my life. Now Dr. Phil's statement about not changing what is not acknowledged is crystal clear.

Legacy/Testimony. With God, all things are possible. This includes creating a new legacy and breaking the curse of divorce. I remember when a man told me I did not know how to love him because I did not have a father in the household. I still don't know if I agree with that in its entirety especially since, at that time, the statement was used as an attack on my character and I resented that. However, God is faithful and I trust that whatever I don't know to do, He will give me the tools, resources and the right man; a man who will love me through my past pain.

Motherhood. The notion that "motherhood changes a woman" is so true. During my pregnancy with my first-born daughter, I knew I would never be the same. This unborn baby would change my life for the better. Before I had the chance to see her newborn face, I knew I would make decisions that would create the "best life" for her. These decisions would mean staying married to her dad, no matter what, to be sure she had a two-parent household, unlike me. Wow! At the age of 28 and as a new mother, here I was still making decisions because of my own "daddy issues." Crazy, right?! Did I know anything about what made a two-parent household so special? Nope, I only knew what "appeared" stable and happy on TV.

Questions. As an adult woman, I have occasionally found myself asking "what if?" What if my father had been present in my life whether in or out of the household? What if we had formed a healthy father/daughter bond? Would I still be married? Who, then, would my husband have been? Also, I have, on occasion, questioned my own judgment in men. I wonder if my father had realized the affect his decisions had in my life, would he have done things differently. I believe it is pointless to put energy into the re-occurring thoughts of what "would of," "should of" and "could of" been done, but instead, celebrate what is now and what is to come.

Access Granted. Now that I have accepted being fatherless as part of my past, my purpose is to share my journey with other women who feel broken and stuck because their father was not in their lives. Someone once said, "Acceptance is the key to change."

New Narrative. Although I have accepted the "I am a fatherless daughter" statement, I am blessed knowing that my heavenly Father, who is my Lord and Savior, has reversed my narrative. I am thankful that His Word reminds me that He will never leave me nor forsake me. I forgive my father and the other men that I allowed to hurt me. My brighter future can begin now that I have accepted that and can now move beyond those five words.

Empowerment. Do not to allow being fatherless to anchor you to past pains or to navigate your present and future existence. Make the choice to acknowledge and accept being a fatherless daughter, without allowing it to have you stuck in victimization.

Final Thought. Sometimes the painful experiences of our past can have you stuck and rehashing all of the wrongs, instead of celebrating all that is right. Healing is not overnight, but I will continue to take intentional steps towards complete healing, walking in forgiveness, avoiding toxic friendships/relationships, and focusing on building a healthy legacy for my children and future generations. I am a fatherless daughter. Accepting five words has changed me and has contributed to breaking the cycle of dysfunction in my life.

Bianca LaTrice Calloway is the founder of Destiny Inspired Consulting, which is a training and leadership development organization designed to help launch individuals to the next level, both personally and professionally. She influences individuals to identify the skills they possess within, through inspirational leadership

A Nickel For Your Thoughts, Dad

By Kathy Marshall

Imaginatively spoken in the voice of my mother, Mary Marshall

I was born on April Fools' Day in 1934, in a little town called Mount Vernon, located in the center of Ohio's vast green cornfields. I was the middle of seven children who were raised by our capable mother, Pearl Williams Carter. Since our birth father, Arthur Carter, was scarcely in our lives, we resided in the house of our grandparents, along with eight other family members. Granddad showed us by example how a man should take care of his family.

I knew at an early age that I did not want to be stuck in that stifling town where the only jobs Black women were allowed to perform involved cooking, laundry or domestic service. Mom encouraged us to shoot for the stars and work hard to become whatever type of person we wanted to be. Being the daughter of an absentee father, I felt motivated to prove to myself and others that I was able to, and worthy of, making a good life for myself.

As a young teenager, I took art lessons by mail, sitting in one corner of the crowded couch to do my art assignments. Drawing portraits was one of my passions, as well as beating other kids at basketball, tennis and marbles.

When I was 15, I got a job at Ringwald's department store as a part-time "window dresser," putting clothes on mannequins in the big store windows. Using my artistic skills, I also painted various signs and backdrops to encourage people to come inside the store and buy those clothes. Sometimes I imagined my father walking by the store windows as I worked, and smiling at my efforts from afar. Many places in the United States were segregated in the 1950s, with African Americans being forced to attend generally substandard schools; but our town's schools were integrated, and we got a decent education. My drawing skills continued to improve, and I became the Art Editor for the 1952 Mount Vernon High School Yearbook, providing all the graphics for that important publication. Miraculously, I was selected to be a part of the Queen's Court at the homecoming dance. I was the first Black girl ever to perform that function in Mount Vernon, where only about one percent of the population was Black.

I believe everything happens for a reason. It was serendipity at a roller skating rink in the nearby town of Zanesville, where I met the man who would become my husband. Thomas Marshall was handsome, tall, athletic, smart, funny, and self-confident. He could carry on an intelligent conversation, and he didn't smoke or drink. Tom and I wrote letters back and forth, for a couple of years, while he was attending Ohio State University College of Medicine in Columbus.

He wanted to marry me, but my goal had always been to wait until I was 21 years of age for marriage. I vowed that I was not going to start having a bunch of babies as a teenager, for that would limit my life's choices, as happened to my mother. The night before the big day in 1955, I dreamed my birth father "gave me away" at our wedding, but that didn't happen. Even so, I hoped dad would approve of my decision.

Sometimes when one door closes, another opens up, bigger and better than the previous one. I received the best wedding present of all: a sweetheart of a father-in-law. Austin Marshall worked on a train in a fancy Pullman Sleeping Car. African American Pullman porters were expected to greet passengers, carry baggage, make up the sleeping berths, serve food and drinks, shine shoes, and keep the cars tidy. Austin's train route was from Columbus, Georgia, where he was born, to St. Louis, Missouri. It continued on to Columbus, Ohio, where Thomas went to school, and we were living. The route ended in Cleveland, Ohio, where Austin lived.

When I became pregnant, my mother-in-law, Daisy, insisted I live with her in Cleveland while Tom completed medical school. That way, when I went into labor, she being a nurse, could be there for the birth. Afterward, she would teach me how to be a good wife and mother.

Well, the icing on the cake was that my father-in-law arranged for me to travel to Cleveland in his Pullman car! He treated me like a queen, just like he would any White person who had bought an expensive ticket on that luxurious conveyance. He escorted me to the spacious berth that was decorated with a crimson velvet sofa and white lace curtains at the window. He served me a sumptuous meal of salad, freshly baked bread, and beef stroganoff on a white porcelain plate. He brought me tea and little cakes on a silver tea service. He even shined my shabby shoes. All the while, Austin bestowed upon me his most beautiful smile. Through him, I finally experienced what it was like to have a father who loved and cared about me.

I learned an important lesson on that fairyland train trip: a father's love and caring does not have to come only from a biological dad. They can come from a stepfather, grandfather, brother, uncle, friend of the family, or a father-in-law. I was lucky to have Austin as my surrogate dad.

For one year, Mama Daisy taught me how to cook, clean and sew. Then Tom whisked me and our daughter away from our Ohio homeland to the West Coast. We ended up having two more children along the way-- Carrie was born in Seattle, Washington, and our son Greg, near Stockton, California, while Tom finished his medical training and military obligations with the US Navy. We moved one last time in 1965, when Tom opened his medical office in South Sacramento. When I began to realize my marriage would not last much longer, I started taking college classes in the mid-1960s to prepare myself to become a working mother. I felt I was emotionally and physically strong enough to handle both important jobs. To ensure my kids always had a father in their lives, I never bad-mouthed Tom in front of them after our divorce. I encouraged my kids to spend regular visits with their dad every other weekend, on holidays, and several weeks during the summer. I, more than anyone, knew how important is was for boy and girl children to have a capable father figure guiding them into adulthood.

To prepare myself for the working world, I completed an Associate of Arts degree in Sociology from Sacramento City College, becoming the first person in my family to graduate from college. I went on to get a Bachelor of Arts in Education from California State University, Sacramento, serving my community as an elementary school teacher in the 1970s.

I was 35 years old when I started my teaching career—a bit late in life. I would have to make a lot more money to earn enough for retirement, so I went back to Sacramento State to earn a Master of Arts degree in Administration, while working full-time as a teacher and mother.

During the next 10 years I was the principal of various elementary schools including Pony Express, Bret Harte, and my favorite, the mostly-minority Camellia Basic Elementary School. I loved interacting with, and helping brown-skinned students reach their academic potential. It was at Camellia, under my watch, when Apple installed 20 brand new computers in 1982 in what became the first Technology Lab in a Sacramento elementary school. Periodically, I wondered whether my father would have been proud of my hard-earned accomplishments.

I gleefully retired in 1989, to begin my second life as a professional artist. I took every art class at Cosumnes River College and settled on watercolor as my medium of choice, because it allowed my vivid color sense to shine brightly. My helpful children encouraged me to open my Mary Marshall Watercolors business in 1995. I enjoyed taking art classes with other like-minded creatives, as well as selling my artworks at various fine art shows around town. I even got a big commission to make 20 paintings for one wing in the massive Antioch Progressive Baptist Church in South Sacramento. Art always made my heart sing and as a retiree, I had all the time in the world to express my thoughts and feelings … and I even earned a bit of pocket change.

Did I say, "pocket change?" One of my favorite extracurricular activities was playing the nickel slot machines. Oh my! It just occurred to me why I only played the nickel machines...

My independent daughter, Kathy, had been consumed with writing about our family history, since the monumental story, "Roots: The Saga of an American Family," aired on television in 1977. She wanted to leave a published legacy about our brave ancestors. Through lots of in-depth research, she managed to do the impossible; she found my mother's enslaved Williams relatives from Maryland, going all the way back to the 1700s. Incredible!

Out of the blue, when I was 62 years of age, Kathy asked, "Mom, where did your father go to work every day and what did he do for a living?" That innocent question shined a harsh spotlight on the saddest depths of my childhood. Truthfully, I only remember meeting my father once, at his mother's house. He gave me a nickel for my fifth birthday. While still a vivid memory even though it occurred so long ago in 1939, that was the extent of "me and my father" time.

Dad was always gone, coming back only long enough to produce eight children in nine years (one died early). By the time I came along, he was rarely there. I heard he was in jail a lot of that time, but I didn't know why. When Kathy asked me to describe my "dearest daddy" moments, I had nothing to say. I did not know whether he was dead or alive, what kind of work he did, what he looked like, or whether he had another family stashed away somewhere. I often wondered, though, whether he ever thought about me, or my brothers and sisters.

It wasn't until 2002 that Kathy and I started using our personal computers for genealogy research, to find out information about our family. All of a sudden, I yearned to find out what happened to my dad. Even though I had a very full life as a Principal; played competitive tennis, golf, and bridge; had a successful art business; and had three wonderful children and three grandchildren of my own, I always kept a little place in my heart for my absentee father.

Could I find out what happened to him using genealogy research? That became an obsession of mine in my last years of life. I scoured vital records offices and historical societies in Ohio; searched the precursor to internet databases; and sent away for official birth and death certificates, all in an effort to find my daddy. At long last, I learned my absentee father passed away in 1994 in Pittsburgh, Pennsylvania, from heart problems. His life story is now memorialized in Kathy's first book, "The Ancestors Are Smiling!"

The nickel my father gave me when I was five years old is my only sweet memory of him. Many times I missed the guidance of a father, but by the examples of a loving grandfather and father-in-law, I experienced the qualities I yearned for in a dad. With the help of a strong mother and mother-in-law, and lots of determination and hard work on my part, I became the person I am today, ironically, not

---

"Even though I had a very full life...I always kept a place in my heart for my absentee dad."

• • • • • • •

---

because of who my absentee father was, but because of who he wasn't.

The next time I go to Cache Creek Casino, I'll play the nickel machines, in Daddy's honor.

Kathy Marshall was a researcher/analyst for the California Highway Patrol for 36 years, and owner/artist of her Kanika African Sculptures art business for 25 years. She has been researching her family roots for four decades, publishing "The Ancestors Are Smiling!" in 2017, which is the first in a series of family history books. She is a mixed media sculptor and author. Visit her at kanikamarshall.com.

Missing You

By Kimberly Bailey

I thought I hadn't missed what I didn't have

until I realized I didn't have you when I should have.

We separated before I was born.

My departure from you was too early for me to mourn

the loss of your presence in mine.

I had no clue who you were, where you were, and why

until that day I learned it was a lie.

At least that's what I believed, until God spoke to me.

It was far from a joke to me.

Standing at an altar with prayed hands, laid hands,
on my face full of tears

From not having you in my life for all 32 of my years.

Somewhere deeply buried was the burning desire for your love.

A little girl, then a wife, still desiring to be the daughter
you'd be proud of.

A beautiful, imperfect, educated, insecure, kind Christian with flaws

Having your features, but never you in the bleachers
giving me applause.

Being blessed with a step, a spiritual, a figure of you,
wasn't the same

Mom left you, you left her, I didn't care who to blame.

I got lost along the way

And all I remembered was not knowing whose I was every day.

I wanted you to show me how not to be shy, but still hold my hand.

I wanted you to help me choose the right, respectable man.

I wanted to be your princess before I became his queen.

I needed you to stop me from being a single mother at 19.

To see pictures of you put a smile on my face.

I prayed the next picture would be one of us, in the same place.

Raising a son without your wisdom was hard.

I prayed he would stay with her and play
with their kids in a backyard.

I nurtured my daughter to be virtuous and valuable to self, first.

Empowered to cultivate a legacy and break the family curse.

I dreamed of time and memories we would make together.

It seemed to be, for the little girl in me, that we would have forever.

Kimberly Bailey is 52 years old. She's been married 21 years and has four children and nine grandchildren. She was born in Los Angeles, California to a single mother of seven. Writing was always her outlet, especially being a shy child in a big family. She has wanted to write a book for (too many) years. When her husband retires from the military, they plan to a book together. Kimberly has written articles for a local magazine, and poetry all my life. She enjoys graphic design, church, community service, mentoring, family gatherings, listening to all kinds of music, and quiet times by herself.

Choices

By Kimberly Biggs Jordan

My father's name was Orlando Lee Biggs, Jr.. Talk about a fine man! Oh, my goodness my father was so fine. He was a tall, light skinned man with an infectious smile and more charisma than the law allowed. As a child he reminded me of Muhammad Ali and I always looked at him as a strong man who would always protect me. He was born in Memphis, Tennessee during a time when racism was rampant and opportunities for Blacks to advance were practically non-existent. At some point during his teen years, most of the Biggs family migrated north to Chicago to take advantage of better opportunities. It was there that he developed his love of being a hustler, Jack Daniels whiskey, gambling, and women.

My father was named after my grandfather, Orlando Lee, who worked for Southern Pacific Railroad. It is said that my grandfather had a woman at every station stop, which would account for my dad's love of women too. Lando, as my dad was called by family members, met my mother in Chicago. I never got the story as to how they met, but I do know that they came from totally different backgrounds and that there was animosity between their families.

When my mother became pregnant with me and then my sister under me, she pushed him into joining the Army so that he could take care of his family and get us out of Chicago. Even though he was married with children, he continued to run the streets, hustling and drinking hard, and women were his vice. The Army eventually gave him orders to report to The Presidio of San Francisco, California and they loaded the station wagon up with our growing family (mommy was pregnant again) and we headed across the country.

Now, remember I said that Daddy was a hustler and hustle he did while in the Army. His MOS (job classification) was a cook. He would bring home cases of cereal, milk, fresh fruit, and meat for the family and he also indulged in black market sales. He rose in the ranks and became the sergeant in charge of the mess hall and began cooking for the officers too. During this time, we moved to Seaside, California and he was stationed at Fort Ord Army Base.

I adored my father and was a daddy's girl. I would shine his boots for cash and he began to teach me how to cook. However, on the homefront he was also a functional, mean alcoholic, whose only interaction with his children outside of teaching me how to cook and mix Bloody Marys, was to be a stern disciplinarian and take us on occasional trips to San Francisco or Dairy Queen.

Life lessons were taught to me by both my parents. I was, and am, a cry baby. I would cry at the "drop of a penny," but my dad tried in his own weird way to toughen me up. He did teach me to stand up for what I believe in and to speak my mind, even if it got me in trouble, which it often did. I learned my lessons well and tried to avoid getting my dad angry at me.

My dad had this thing he did when he was drunk and mad at the world. He would take his finger and hit us on the tip of the nose, while he enunciated each word of whatever he was berating us about. I hated that finger with a purple passion. To this day if someone points their finger at me they are warned that it could be all bad for them if they don't remove it. I would get the finger on the nose mainly about my grades. Mind you, I was an honor student but didn't excel in math, which was my dad's favorite subject. He gave me a complex about math that I still have today.

I learned as a child to make myself into a small package and stay out of his sight when he would come home drunk. Many nights he would come home after being in the streets doing whatever he was doing and I would hear him begging my mom to fix him something to eat. My mom's response was "you should have eaten where you were at." I knew within minutes he would come into my room and get me up to fix him some eggs over easy and a bowl of chili. The crazy thing is, he would fall asleep with his face in the bowl of chili.

My father would yell at us, ordering us around like we were his soldiers, but he didn't always have to speak to issue an order. I remember one time he was instructing me on how to mow the lawn. Our next-door neighbor, Mr. Ziegler came over and told me to put the mulch in the flower beds. My dad gave me a look that said "you better not," and I didn't because even though I loved my dad, I was afraid of him. He ruled with an iron fist and his butt whoopings I can still feel today when I think about them. It wasn't easy growing up with him and I know my choices in men and my life's direction took the turns they did, because of him. Nights when he would come home drunk, I would lay in bed listening to my parents argue and it was then that I vowed that when I got older and had children, I would not have them grow up in a home with an alcoholic.

His alcoholism really affected me because I didn't understand. He seemed to have it all together. He was admired by his peers and officers in the military. He was an amazing cook and he provided an upper middle-class lifestyle for his family. How could he be so unhappy? I really thought about that during the times he would sit at the kitchen table with his head down crying and rubbing his head. As a child I didn't understand about addictions. It wasn't until years later and my father got sick and passed away that I understood his unhappiness with his life.

I realized at his funeral, that most of his unhappiness stemmed from his life choices. He became a father at a young age and he never accepted that the lifestyle he truly wanted would never be his reality. He wanted to run the streets, shoot dice, drink, and be a player. I sat there in that chapel, where armed security was there per his family, because of actions from certain people in my immediate family. I wondered how life had gotten turned around so bad for him. He had been sprayed with Agent Orange in Vietnam and he eventually developed kidney failure. He was estranged from his five children with my mother and I was stunned to learn that very few people in Colorado Springs where he lived, even knew of our existence.

My heart was broken as I sat there reflecting on my own choices and how they had mirrored his. Every man I had been with had had some form of addiction. The gay father of my two eldest children sat next to me in the pew, he was addicted to drugs and alcohol. Later in life, the father of my youngest daughter was a functional alcoholic and drug addict.

What happened to my childhood vow to never have my children live with an alcoholic? I had my own battles with addiction that I had to face. One of my addictions was seeking the love and approval of men who had addictive personalities because I saw a little bit of my father in them. See, when I was 14 years old my parents divorced, and my father turned his back on his family. He acted as though we didn't exist. This one action alone devastated me, because I loved my dad no matter who he was or how he was. I just loved him. How could he deny us and leave us to struggle through life, while he provided for and took care of my younger brother by another woman? I started seeking that love in all the wrong men.

Today as I think back on it with tears in my eyes, I think about how different life would have been had my dad faced his fears and dealt with his addiction. I think about the times when he was sick and my mother, my sister and I went to him at different times, to help take care of him despite how he treated us and denied us. I have a recording that I made for him in the '80s asking him a lot of questions about his actions. I expressed to him how his actions affected my life. He listened to it and never responded. I just wanted him to understand the domino effect of his unhappiness and addiction on myself and my siblings. I never got that closure.

At his funeral, his politically correct daughter, the one he taught to stand up tall and straight, the one he taught to cook and speak up for her beliefs and speak her mind, stood before his family and friends and spoke about the man that I had always looked up to, who reminded me so much of Muhammad Ali. I quoted my favorite bible scripture, Ecclesiastes 3:1-8, which begins with "There is a time for everything, and a season for every activity under heaven" and I forgave my father for all he had done to me.

" I pray today that my father has found his peace and that the wounds of his past have healed. His children are still healing..."

I pray today that my father has found his peace and that the wounds of his past have healed. His children are still healing, his children are still fighting various addictions and as for me, I still love my father despite it all. Life is all about the choices we make and my dad's choices affected his six children and his 50 grand children and great grandchildren.

It's time to break the generational curse. The time and season has come for Kimberly to heal and break the chains of addiction that has visited my father and my family. I am still, and always will be, a daddy's girl and at 60 years old, I am still seeking that love I so desperately wanted from my father. Today, because I want to change how my own children and grandchildren deal with life and relationships, I am embracing change and accepting who I am and the consequences of my own life choices.

If I could speak to my father today, I would say "Daddy, I'm sorry you were so unhappy in life, and even though you thought no one loved you, just know I have always loved you and always will."

Kimberly Biggs Jordan developed her love of reading, writing and playing with words early in life. They took her to places the Army hadn't stationed her father to and they became an escape for her imagination to run free. Kimberly's passion for the community has led her to become a community advocate for youth, the Inspired Butterfly a Motivational Speaker, who uses her real-life stories of triumphs and failures to help motivate and encourage women and young girls. As an author, Kimberly writes short stories, poetry and spoken word, which she hopes to return to performing soon. The stories and poetry that she writes, reflects her 60 years of life experiences and the people in them. Her work has been included in several anthologies, including "Our Black Mothers, Brave Bold and Beautiful," that features a story about her mother, called "True Grace." Kimberly said the story "Choices," about her father, was one of the most emotional pieces she has ever written.

Daddy Issues

Healing Exercise

In her piece "His Loss...," Genoa M. Barrow writes about a letter her good friend once wrote to her father, pouring out her desire to have a better relationship with him. Bianca LaTrice Calloway also mentions a letter she wrote to her father in her piece, "Acceptance of Five Words: A Fatherless Daughter," in which she shares with him how his absence was impacting her. If you could write a letter to the man who fathered you, what would you say? If he's never been in your life, what questions would you have for him? If he was there, but still "wasn't present," what would you want/need him to hear?

Daddy Issues

Healing Exercise

Redefining You Therapy
3105 1st Avenue, Suite A
Sacramento, California 95817
www.RedefiningYouTherapy.com

REDEFINING YOUTHERAPY

Provides:

- Short-Term Counseling (Individual and Family)
- Anger Management Classes
- Professional and Therapeutic Supervised Visitation
- Safe Exchange

Accepts EAP Insurance
Referrals from The Soldier's Project and
California Victims Compensation
Listed on the Sacramento Superior Court Resource List
Contracted with Sacramento County Child Protective
Services (CPS) for
Short-Term Counseling and Anger Management

*Sliding Scale Available
Evening and Weekend hours by appointment

Ola Adams-Best, LCSW
(916) 956-6232

Peter W. Best, MSWI
(916) 216-1166

Flojaune G. Cofer
PhD, MPH

Director of State Policy & Research

Public Health Advocates

PO Box 2309 Davis, CA 95617

[w] 844.962.5900, x230

[m] 404.668.0735

PHAdvocates.org

~

Host of the TRG 5K Resolution race/walk

Held annually in Sacramento, California
in January

trg5kresolution.org

SHARE YOUR STORY IN

DADDY ISSUES:
BLACK WOMEN SPEAKING
TRUTH & HEALING WOUNDS
VOLUME 2

FOR MORE INFORMATION
& SUBMISSION GUIDELINES

EMAIL

DADDYISSUESANTHOLOGY@GMAIL.COM

UNLIMITED

56915568R00057

Made in the USA
Columbia, SC
03 May 2019